FAMILY IS ALWAYS FIRST

INSIGHTS FOR NURTURING LASTING RELATIONSHIPS

Sheetal Kumar Niranjan

1

FAMILY IS ALWAYS FIRST

Insights for nurturing lasting relationships

Sheetal Kumar Niranjan

Dedication

This book is a tribute to my loving family. I will never forget your love, encouragement, and the countless moments we've shared. Because of your presence in my life, I've been able to embark on this journey. Thank you for being my constant source of strength and inspiration and yes "Family is always First".

With all my love,

Sheetal Kumar Niranjan

Table of Contents

Introduction

"Family is not an important thing. It's everything."

- Michael J. Fox

This book aims to provide practical advice and insights into family psychology. It focuses on understanding and addressing the needs of husbands, wives, children, and grandparents. Families can build stronger, more harmonious relationships by gaining a deeper understanding of each other's perspectives and needs.

Family dynamics are essential in shaping our emotional well-being and overall happiness. Understanding these dynamics helps us navigate conflicts, communicate effectively, and support each other meaningfully.

The book is divided into four parts:
- Understanding the husband's perspective
- Understanding the wife's perspective
- Understanding the child's perspective

- Understanding the grandparents' perspective

Each part is a separate chapter that delve into specific aspects of each family member's needs and how to address them.

Chapter 1: Understanding the Husband's Perspective

"I sustain myself with the love of family."

- Maya Angelou

Source Image: by Daniela Dimitrova from Pixabay.com

Communication Needs

The Importance of Clear Communication

Clear communication is essential for long lasting and healthy relationships. It involves expressing thoughts, feelings and needs in a way that the other person quickly understands.

In the early days of married life, introverted husbands, who have the best intentions but are often shy, may find it hard to express themselves. It takes them time to open up and express themselves freely because they want to establish trust and a strong bond with their wife. This is when the wife needs to be patient and should look for ways to have deeper, more meaningful conversations with the husband. This helps establish an emotional connection, which helps establish a strong relationship.

Extrovert husbands usually find it easy to communicate. On the flip side, they may be overbearing to their wives and end up listening less but talking more. Here, it is critical to remind each other to find the right balance so that mutual respect is maintained.

As time goes by, life becomes busy, and there are very few opportunities for deep conversations. This is when taking time out to be with each other and to have these conversations becomes of paramount importance. It is so easy for both the husband and wife to get lost in their own little worlds, and it is very important to strengthen that same emotional bond from time to time.

Common Misunderstandings

Misunderstandings often arise from assumptions and misinterpretations. Husbands can sometimes feel that not everything needs to be discussed with the wife, as it may not have much to do with family affairs. Making decisions without consulting the wife, thinking she would largely be in line with the decision, can prove to be very detrimental. The wife feels undervalued, not respected, and demotivated. The husband could go through the same situation, too, and feel exactly the same.

These feelings may slowly grow over time, and once patience is lost, it eventually leads to conflicts and resentment if not addressed early. Open communication is, therefore, key to avoiding such situations. Everything should be discussed, and each other's opinions definitely matter and should be considered.

How to Express Needs and Feelings Effectively

- Use "I" statements to express feelings. This clearly demonstrates that you mean what you say.
- Be specific about needs and expectations. Explain the intent in the most straightforward way you can, enhancing your chances of better understanding.

- Practing active listening helps understand your partner's perspective. This requires patience and understanding, which comes with building trust and respect for each other

Emotional Support

What Emotional Support Looks Like for Men

Men often seek emotional support through actions rather than words. To elaborate, men could be more expressive of their feelings through words, but these are conveyed through actions. Simple actions that show that a husband cares are to be picked up by the wife. When they offer to help and go beyond their normal duties, that's when they are most expressive and appreciative or only trying to reciprocate their wife's efforts. It is coming from a place of respect and love.

In return, it is often the same things that are expected. They appreciate gestures that show understanding and care. Action that makes them understand the wife's intent is enough for the husband to feel appreciated and loved. They want to be heard and understood because there is more to life than just hard work and regular stressors. The strong man portrayal, whose emotions are in check and who is not vulnerable, is a huge myth. We all have our weaknesses, and men are no exception to this. If they are to set ambitious goals in life, it comes with the confidence that the family is backing and routing for their success. Lack of emotional support can so easily break a man, and with the proper support, they can also do wonders.

How to Provide It

- Offer practical help and encouragement. Keeping nudging men to strive for more and not settle for mediocrity is critical.
- Be patient and non-judgmental when they express emotions and create a safe space for vulnerability. This helps them be themselves, and the more they identify with themselves, the more confident, ambitious, and self-assured they will be. This is essential to leading a great family life because earning money through a job is just an enabler to a better lifestyle.

However, one needs to function with freedom and clarity to lead a quality life.

The Role of Empathy and Understanding

Empathy involves putting yourself in your partner's shoes and understanding their emotions. We all go through so much in our lives, and often, what seems trivial may mean the world to our partner. Husbands and wives are usually very different, and it is beautiful. It gives them plenty of opportunities to learn from one another and understand each other at a profound level because true unity is about learning to stay together despite being the opposites of one another and yet finding ways and reasons to build a strong emotional bond and foster a supportive environment for one another.

Respect and Appreciation

The Need for Respect in a Relationship

Respect is essential for a healthy relationship. It involves acknowledging your partner's worth and treating them with kindness and consideration. Sometimes, things are taken for granted, and therefore, effort does not meet the right level of appreciation. Understanding each other's sacrifices, dedication to the family, and the bond everybody shares is critical. Actions speak louder than words, and that's what helps garner respect. The feeling of appreciation only comes when you feel respect for each other.

How to Show Appreciation

- Express gratitude for your partner's efforts and qualities. I express gratitude to everyone and everything in life. This helps you live in peace with yourself, and it rubs off on the family as well. Show that you care and be sincere about it. Words are powerful and often kind, and understanding is all that partners expect from each other.

- Celebrate their achievements, big or small. Life has to be about celebrating small and big achievements. It keeps everybody motivated and wanting to do more. Take a pause to live in the present and soak it all in. It's not always about what's ahead. Still, it is also about acknowledging the achievements and being thankful to have lived in the moment and created memories that last a lifetime.

- Show interest in their passions and hobbies. It's not always about "What's in it for me?". It should be about how we can spend quality time together and have the attitude to explore something that you may not like or have yet to understand in the past. Again, create memories, and they're always better created together. Who knows? You may find a new passion or interest that you never felt before.

Recognizing and Valuing Contributions

Each partner contributes uniquely to the relationship. Recognizing and valuing these contributions fosters a sense of partnership and mutual respect, which is the true secret to a long-lasting relationship. If we can follow this culture in the office, why not at home? We are, after all, working together on a bigger project called "Marriage," and it is important that both of you feel the need and hunger to succeed together in this endeavour.

Shared Interests and Activities

Importance of Spending Time Together

Spending quality time together strengthens the relationship and creates lasting memories. It helps partners connect on a deeper level. It is only when deep conversations happen that both of them can understand each other better. Thoughts can be exchanged; ideas can be floated around and debated about, leading to camaraderie and admiration for one another. There are so many great qualities to discover in each other, which requires quality time spent with each other. A lot of our behaviour does rub off on our partners and often positively influences them.

Finding Common Interests

Identify activities that both partners enjoy. This could include hobbies, sports, or cultural events. Sharing a common love for trying different cuisines, travelling and planning a trip together, watching movies, listening to songs, playing sports, working out in the gym together, and following a healthy diet plan together—there is so much to do together, and the list is just endless. Living in the moment and feeling the experience is essential, as these memories are created together for a lifetime.

Balancing Individual and Shared Activities

While shared activities are important, it's also essential to maintain individual interests. This balance ensures personal growth and prevents dependency. It is crucial to understand and respect each other's space and to allow the partner to find their "me time". It cannot be that both partners would enjoy all the activities that perhaps only one of them enjoys, and therefore, it is crucial to identify such activities and enjoy them alone. The other partner should understand this and allow their partner to enjoy the individual activity, encouraging them to let it happen more frequently. By giving enough freedom to one

another, they can both be happy and stay in a
positive state of mind.

Intimacy and Affection

Understanding Different Forms of Intimacy

It is essential to understand that intimacy goes beyond physical affection. It includes emotional and intellectual intimacy as well. Contrary to popular belief, husbands, or men in general, need emotional support more than wives, if not equally. They like to be heard and understood better. Men have a vulnerable side, and it is perfectly okay for them to feel vulnerable. Life throws many challenges, and it can be very demanding, as they are expected to show a bold face and give the impression that they are always in control of every situation. This is further from the truth. Predominantly being the family's primary caregiver, guardian, or provider is a challenging job. Therefore, everybody in the household must support each other and reduce the family pressures on one another. Big or small decisions need to be discussed and taken, keeping the family's interests in mind.

The Role of Physical Affection

Physical touch is a powerful way to express love and affection. The importance of it is often felt when there is a lack of it. It can include holding hands, hugging, or cuddling. This needs to be improved among middle-aged or older couples and fixed immediately. By holding each other, hugging each other, or cuddling each other, it has been seen that endorphins are released in each other's bodies, helping them to calm down and feel good about each other. It helps build a strong bond with one another, and most of the time, you do not even have to say a single word to feel the way you feel and build that understanding with each other. It helps people communicate non-verbally with each other, and that is powerful. Therefore, take every opportunity to feel physical affection more often and build a strong bond.

Building a Strong Emotional Connection

Emotional intimacy involves sharing thoughts, dreams, and fears. It requires vulnerability and trust, built over time through consistent effort. Spend time with each other. Communicate with one another at a very deep level. Feel the connection, and give it time to nurture and grow without feeling rushed. Identify activities that both of you enjoy doing and explore them more often. Rediscover each other from time to time. Learn from each other and grow wiser together.

Chapter 2: Understanding the Wife's Perspective

"Ohana means family. Family means no one gets left behind or forgotten."

- Lilo and Stitch

Source Image: by Neil Dodhia from Pixabay.com

Emotional Connection

Importance of Emotional Intimacy

Emotional intimacy is needed for strong relationship. It involves understanding and validating each other's emotions. Women are much more emotional than men; like men, they want to be heard and understood. Often, newlywed women need a lot of support as they want to blend in with everybody in their new home. To leave behind their family and home to start their new family is quite a challenge, and it is up to the husband and the rest of his family members to provide care and comfort to his wife. Hormonal changes within women and the period cycles often take a toll on them, as they face a lot of mood swings. Husbands need to understand this, be patient and empathetic about it, and not be overbearing on their wives at these times.

How to Build and Maintain Emotional Connection

- Share your feelings openly and honestly. There is no reason to hold back feelings; it is always best to express them as openly and clearly as possible. This helps build a powerful bond in the long run.
- Be present and attentive during conversations. I can't emphasize this enough. It is very important to be available mentally and physically and to understand each other through verbal communication and nonverbal cues.
- Show empathy and understanding. Understanding what each other is going through in their lives and expressing empathy is crucial, as it helps them remain in a positive frame of mind and have a positive outlook on things. Patience is key.

Recognizing Emotional Needs

Recognize and address your partner's emotional needs. This includes providing comfort, support, and reassurance. Being there for each other and looking out for each other is the secret to a long-lasting relationship. Mutual respect and understanding of the efforts in running the show, so to speak, are to be acknowledged and appreciated by both. Gratitude for one another is also a key ingredient in helping maintain positive emotions. Listening to each other, having healthy conversations, feeling valued, and exchanging ideas or thoughts to improve the current situation all contribute to emotional wellness.

Support and Partnership

What Support Looks Like for Women

Women often seek emotional and practical support. This includes being listened to, understood, and assisted in daily tasks. I have already expressed my thoughts on emotional support in the previous chapter. Practical support means support with some household chores and small and timely assistance with simple tasks to which husbands can contribute and reduce the wife's workload. Tasks such as hanging the clothes on the line to allow them to dry, cutting vegetables or washing them, arranging things, and putting them back in their place are some that husbands can support. This combination of emotional empathy and practical assistance makes them feel valued and supported. When a partner listens attentively and shares the load of daily chores, it strengthens the relationship by fostering a sense of partnership and mutual care, leading to a happier, more balanced home life.

Being a True Partner

A true partnership involves sharing responsibilities and decision-making. It starts with both partners having mutual respect for one another and the willingness to cooperate and assist one another. With the mindset that no work or responsibility is to be seen as big or small but to be treated equally, the duties can be divided based on expertise in that particular area or the sheer interest to learn and perform it. Duties can also be interchanged once they begin to feel dull and mundane. When it comes to decision-making, both of them or the entire family need to come together, discuss the pros and cons, and then make a final decision that suits everyone. This helps build trust and faith in one another, creating a harmonious environment.

Appreciation and Validation

The Need for Appreciation

Appreciation and gratitude play vital roles in forming a healthy relationship. They involve recognizing and valuing your partner's efforts and contributions.

How to Validate Feelings and Efforts

- Acknowledge your partner's feelings without judgment. Allowing each partner to express how they feel and why they feel is a huge part of communicating well with the partner. This helps us understand partners' perspectives better and allows us to be open about things with proper understanding.
- Express gratitude for their efforts and sacrifices. As mentioned in an earlier chapter, expressing gratitude towards everyone and everything in life helps you

live in peace with yourself and rubs off on the family. Show that you care and be sincere about it. Words are powerful and often kind words, and understanding is all that partners expect from each other.

- Celebrate their successes and achievements. As mentioned in an earlier chapter, life has to be about celebrating small and big achievements. It is what keeps everybody motivated and wanting to do more. Take a pause to live in the present and soak it all in. It's not always about what's ahead, but it is also about acknowledging the achievements and being thankful to have been able to live in the moment and create memories that last a lifetime.

Recognizing and Celebrating Successes

Celebrate milestones and achievements together. It is vital to make it a point to celebrate birthdays, anniversaries, and other special occasions or achievements without holding back. Of course, it could be a private celebration with

the family, but this is crucial in building a strong
bond and expressing care and joy for one
another.

Communication and Understanding

Effective Communication Strategies

Effective communication involves expressing thoughts and feelings clearly and respectfully. Knowing whether the person or people hearing you can understand you entirely is essential to avoiding confusion. Often, it is easy to assume that the person listening to you has understood everything when that may not be the case. It is, therefore, essential to communicate in a way that is easily understood by others and to be as clear as possible. The same works in family dynamics. It is best to share the context of what is being said and how the statement will be received. Contextual clarity is super important. Nonverbal cues are also quickly picked up by partners without a word being spoken. This, of course, results from knowing and understanding each other very closely.

Active Listening and Empathy

Active listening involves fully concentrating, understanding, and responding to your partner. Empathy involves understanding and sharing your feelings. Being transparent and open with each other helps develop a better experience. Understanding when to speak, what to speak, and how to speak are vital attributes that partners need to exercise with each other. Being emotionally intelligent helps develop a deep bond and helps have deep conversations more often.

Resolving Conflicts Constructively

- Address conflicts calmly and respectfully. Spend time understanding rather than rushing through or reaching a conclusion. Refrain from interfering because it can often change the context of the conflict, and matters can only get worse from where they started. One-on-one discussion and resolution are vital.
- Focus on finding solutions rather than blaming. The goal is to end the conflict and

not worsen it. Blaming each other only worsens the situation, but exhibiting patience and knowing that nobody is perfect should tune the mind to look for solutions. Starting with why there is a conflict, how both of you are feeling, whether you wish to continue to feel this way, and how to get out of that feeling is how the situation needs to be assessed. This helps resolve conflicts faster.

- Compromise and find common ground. If a resolution is not possible, it is best to find a middle ground and for both partners to come to a compromise that works for both of them.

Affection and Romance

Importance of Romance in a Relationship

Romance is crucial in a relationship because it keeps the emotional connection solid and vibrant. Acts of romance, such as complimenting, planning surprise dates, or expressing affection, make partners feel cherished and valued. It breaks the monotony of daily routines, adding excitement and intimacy. Romance fosters closeness and rekindles the passion that initially brought the couple together. It helps build a deeper bond, ensuring both partners feel loved and appreciated. Regular romantic gestures show commitment and effort, reinforcing the strength and longevity of the relationship.

Ways to Show Affection

- Plan surprise dates or getaways. Favourite restaurants, places, activities, or planning something different that has never been tried before are good options. Everybody has their unique styles and tastes. Spending quality time together should be the primary objective.

- Write love notes or messages. If you find it hard, look it up on the internet, and you can find several beautiful quotes or notes that you can use. Remember, how the partner feels matters, not exactly the words themselves.
- Express love through small, thoughtful gestures. Buying gifts for one another is an excellent way. Appreciating and pampering your partner more often and making them feel valued is the way to go. Complement each other. Look good for each other. Dress well. Smell well. There is so much each of you can do.

Keeping the Spark Alive

Maintain a sense of adventure and spontaneity. Continuously find new ways to connect and keep the romance alive. Keep reinventing yourselves, and don't grow stale. Try new experiences, places to eat, and places you have never visited. Find the fun activities that both of you enjoy and indulge in them.

Chapter 3: Understanding the Child's Perspective

"It is the smile of a child, the love of a mother, the joy of a father, the togetherness of a family."

- Menacheim Begin

Source Image: by Bess Hamiti from Pixabay.com

Love and Affection

The Child's Need for Love

Children need unconditional love and affection to feel secure and valued. They feel most comfortable and confident when they get their family's encouragement and support. It's best not to be overly critical of mistakes and instead explain adequately how to avoid them next time. It is crucial to allow them to thrive by mentoring them in various aspects of life and at different stages of their lives. It's essential to understand them and then nurture them so they can lead a fulfilling life. All of this has to come from a place of love and gratitude. They are, after all, the blessings in any parent's life.

Ways to Show Affection

- Spend quality time together, perform activities together, be there for them when they need you, teach them things you know and what you want them to learn, and pick one day of the week as a family day and be with them. There are loads of things that can be done together. Create memories together. Have a blast.

- Give hugs and verbal affirmations. Hugs have a soothing effect, and they help build strong bonds together as they create a sense of security and trust. Children are often very prone to mood swings, and for parents, it's not easy dealing with that. Telling them stories of how their parents went about their childhood and the different coping mechanisms is precious information to pass on to children. It builds their confidence and a sense of stability as they understand that everybody faces ups and downs. Encouraging words do wonders for children. Positive affirmations help reinforce their belief in themselves.

- Show interest in their activities and interests. Parents need to stay curious and ready to explore their child's or children's worlds. Participating with them in activities helps us spend quality time with them, and this is something that children look forward to. By understanding their interests, parents can be enablers, make the relevant arrangements, and create opportunities for them to explore and thrive. Discovering the child's or children's talents is crucial, and based on their interests, the right coaching or guidance can be provided to nurture further and grow their abilities.

Building a Secure Attachment

A secure attachment forms the foundation for healthy emotional development. It involves consistent, responsive caregiving. Spending time with children should be a mandate for every parent. Being their first role models, it is essential to set the proper examples for them, as children learn from their parents the most, especially in their formative years. As they grow older, they look for parents to treat them as friends and respectfully. It is okay for parents to be strict or lenient as the situation demands and to expect certain behaviours from their children.

Communication and Understanding

Listening to Your Child

Listen actively to your child's thoughts and feelings. Show that you value their opinions and experiences. There is often so much to learn from them. Including them in decision-making helps them gain confidence and a better understanding of the topic of discussion. The child must feel that the parents are approachable and will listen to everything the child says without being judgmental or jumping to conclusions. Children need to know that there is somebody to listen to them.

Encouraging Open Communication

Creating an open and non-judgmental environment makes the child feel comfortable sharing everything with the parents. This is so essential for the child's mental health and confidence-building. It helps children and parents build a solid trust and belief system. Open communication is the need of the hour as children face so many pressures and stressful situations daily, and they will need to speak it out to feel better.

Understanding Their Feelings and Needs

Recognize and validate your child's emotions. Help them understand and express their feelings healthily, and try to orient them to think positively. A positive attitude and mindset towards everything will help them keep their emotions in check and not feel disappointed when things don't go their way. It is essential to help them understand their feelings and react appropriately. Parents need to help them grow their emotional intelligence, and that comes from understanding how the world works and how situations are to be handled.

Support and Encouragement

Providing Emotional and Moral Support

Please support your child through challenges and celebrate their achievements. Provide encouragement and reassurance through words and actions. Helping children develop and grow their emotional intelligence is necessary. It helps them understand situations better and react to them accordingly. Sharing stories and anecdotes about situations parents have faced and handled will enhance children's understanding.

Talking about celebrating achievements, big or small, should be more frequent. Celebrations help boost the mood and enhance a positive outlook on life. It helps build children's confidence and encourages them to strive for more.

Encouraging Interests and Talents

Support your child's interests and talents.
Provide opportunities for them to explore and
develop their skills. Discovering the child's or
children's talents early is crucial, and based on
their interests, the right coaching or guidance
can be provided to nurture further, grow their
talents, and enhance their skill levels. This will
provide them with many opportunities to explore
and discover themselves and to shape their
personalities.

Helping with Challenges and Stress

Help your child manage stress and overcome
challenges. Discussing stressors with children and
sharing thoughts and input on how to cope with
them is important. Sharing stories and anecdotes
about situations parents have faced and handled
will enhance children's understanding. It is
important to give children the freedom to
express themselves freely without holding back,
and for that, they need to know that their parents
are approachable. Open conversations are
essential for good mental and emotional health.

Discipline and Boundaries

Importance of Consistent Discipline

Consistent discipline is crucial because it helps children understand what is expected of them. When rules are clear and consistently enforced, kids know what behaviours are acceptable and what will lead to consequences. This makes them feel safe and secure, as they can predict how their parents will respond. Consistent discipline teaches responsibility, helps develop self-control, and promotes good behaviour. It also shows that parents care enough to guide them and set boundaries. Knowing the limits and having a routine make the world more understandable and less confusing for children.

Setting Healthy Boundaries

Establish clear, reasonable boundaries that respect the child's autonomy while ensuring safety and respect. It is important for parents not to be very intrusive in the lives of their children but, at the same time, set up safety nets for them and be aware of what's going on at all times. Having open conversations with each other gives them enough confidence. It reinforces their belief in the safety mechanisms set up for children.

Balancing Authority and Freedom

Balancing discipline with freedom is good for encouraging independence. Allowing children to make choices within established boundaries gives them autonomy and a sense of control without parents being overbearing on their children. Having healthy conversations provides clarity to both parties. Every household should have rules for everybody to follow, which should allow each family member enough autonomy and freedom to work with.

Quality Time and Involvement

The Importance of Quality Time

Quality time spent together helps strengthen the parent-child bond. It provides opportunities for each of them to stay connected and share experiences. Therefore, it becomes vital to take time off and go on vacations where time can be spent together. Planning activities like playing games or sports together each week also helps. There are loads of things that can be done and plenty of opportunities to explore new things.

Engaging in Activities Together

Participate in activities that both you and your child enjoy. This could include hobbies, sports, or educational projects. Identify common interests and pursue them together. It's all about spending time with one another and, in the process, understanding each other in depth. Supporting each other at various phases of life is essential;

hence, developing a solid bond plays a considerable role.

Another thing that works well is to gamify daily routines and mundane tasks and give each other points when something is achieved. At the end of the month or week, the person with the most points will decide where the family goes to eat, which outing place to visit, which concert to attend, etc. There is so much that can be done.

Being Involved in Their Lives

When parents are involved, children feel loved, valued, and supported. This involvement includes attending school events, helping with homework, playing together, and discussing their day. It shows that parents care about their interests, successes, and challenges. This active participation boosts a child's confidence and self-esteem, knowing they have a dependable support system. It also strengthens the parent-child bond, making children feel secure and understood. Parent's interest in their world creates a sense of belonging. It encourages open communication, helping them thrive emotionally and socially.

Chapter 4: Understanding the Grandparents' Perspective

"Nobody can do for little children what grandparents do. Grandparents sort of sprinkle stardust over the lives of little children."

- Alex Haley

Source Image: by Sasin Tipchai from Pixabay.com

Wisdom and Experience

The Value of Grandparents' Wisdom

Grandparents offer a wealth of knowledge and experience. Their life lessons can guide and enrich their grandchildren's or children's lives. One can't be aware of or knowledgeable about everything. When it comes to matters of the home, often experience in handling situations seems easier to grandparents as they would have seen these for the longest of times compared to anybody at home. Also, the knowledge gained is precious and can be easily passed on to the next generation.

How They Can Share Their Experiences

- Tell stories about their own lives and family history. Often a favourite activity for grandchildren, hearing stories of the family history and how life was a couple of decades ago intrigues young minds. It makes grandchildren think about and appreciate the various aspects of life. It is now, and I learned from both of these life timelines. Knowing the family heritage and lineage needs to be passed on from generation to generation, as there are always significant learnings and inspirational aspects that one can learn from.

- Learning practical skills and hobbies from grandparents may mean keeping some dying skills or traditions alive. For example, cooking a specific traditional dish or acquiring knowledge of the medicinal properties of herbs and leaves are skills to learn from grandparents, both to keep the practice alive and to reap the benefits of applying those skills for the greater good. It can often be observed that grandparents would have led and are continuing to lead a healthier lifestyle simply because they would have been more active and energetic compared to the sedentary lifestyles of most people today. Adopting healthy practices will help parents and children be more nutritious and active.

- Grandparents must offer advice and guidance when asked by children or grandchildren. It is also important for children and grandchildren to seek advice from grandparents and not feel that grandparents will come up with old ideas that don't really mean much in today's times. The fact that they would have seen and experienced a lot in their lives means that there is definitely something for everyone to learn.

Respecting Their Contributions

The help and support grandparents provide should be acknowledged and appreciated. Their selfless acts and giving attitude are often underrated and not recognized. They always look out for the family and keep the family interests ahead of their interests. It is a massive advantage for a family where the grandparents live with the parents and children. They pick up many daily household chores, which helps lessen the burden on everyone else. No amount of gratitude or respect is ever enough to acknowledge them.

Therefore, it becomes the duty of the other family members to look out for and care for them. Simple deeds like cooking, ordering their favourite food, or visiting their favourite places are often what make them happy.

Emotional Bonds

Importance of Maintaining Emotional Bonds with Grandchildren

Strong emotional bonds between grandparents and grandchildren provide a sense of security and continuity among each other. Children often learn a lot from their grandparents and are influenced by them. More often than not, children spend more time with their grandparents, as parents are generally busy. Therefore, it is also up to the grandparents to help shape the grandchildren's personalities and nurture them. Helping them make decisions by understanding right and wrong and sharing suggestions benefits the grandchildren. Getting involved and participating with grandchildren in their various hobbies or interests and explaining the family dynamics, traditions, and rituals are vital, and the grandparents often do a great job at that.

Activities and Traditions to Strengthen Bonds

- Engaging in shared hobbies or interests helps grandparents and grandchildren spend time together, having fun and enjoying themselves in the process.
- Establishing family traditions and rituals comes easily to grandparents, who are often more patient and diligent in explaining the intricate details so that the grandchildren find them intriguing and think they must adopt them.

Providing Emotional Support

Grandparents can offer emotional support by being good listeners, offering comfort, and providing a different perspective. Their patience is simply unmatched. Their words of wisdom and the assurance they provide by saying, "Everything is going to be okay", are massive emotionally supportive lines. Seeing them around is reassuring and creates a positive vibe at home.

Role in Family Dynamics

Understanding Their Role in the Family

Grandparents play a vital role in family dynamics, offering support, wisdom, and stability. They are solid pillars of support for any family, and they play their role perfectly. They spend the most time with grandchildren and play a crucial role in shaping their personalities. They always lend an ear to understand and respond accordingly to their children. They often have a calming effect on the family dynamic.

Balancing Involvement and Respecting Boundaries

Grandparents should be involved in family activities and decisions while respecting the parents' primary role and offering support without overstepping or undermining the parents' authority. This helps maintain harmony at home and allows them to share a cordial relationship.

Supporting Their Adult Children

- Providing emotional and practical support to their children is vital and often the need of the hour. It is easy for anybody to feel vulnerable and emotionally drained in a fast-paced world, and for the children to know that they have somebody to listen to them can do wonders for their confidence.
- Grandparents must respect their children's parenting choices and offer advice only when asked. That's when respect and harmony can easily be maintained at home.
- They are being a source of stability and reassurance. Everybody needs a shoulder to lean on, and who better than our parents? Their words of wisdom and timely advice are what every family needs and are often underrated, which is unfortunate.

Legacy and Traditions

Passing Down Family Traditions

Grandparents are vital to preserving and passing down family traditions and values. Teachings passed down in the form of stories and anecdotes are easy to remember, and their significance can be easily understood. Maintaining any age-old artefacts and timely handover of the same to the next generation helps pass them on from generation to generation.

Sharing Family History and Stories

- Telling stories about family history and ancestors helps us understand the family legacy across generations. This is important for families across nations with a strong family legacy and history.
- Keeping family albums and memorabilia is essential, as those memories are priceless. It also becomes imperative for the next

generation of family members to maintain these and ensure that they get passed on from generation to generation.

- For grandparents, celebrating cultural heritage and traditions is a way to pass down values, stories, and customs that define their family's identity. Sharing traditional foods, holidays, and rituals connects generations. It allows grandparents to impart wisdom and life lessons, helping grandchildren understand their roots and history.

Creating Lasting Memories

Grandparents create special memories with grandchildren through shared experiences, celebrations, and traditions. Celebrations strengthen family bonds and create cherished memories. Grandparents take pride in seeing their heritage live on, ensuring that future generations respect and remember their culture and traditions, and preserving a legacy that enriches the family's collective experience.

Conclusion

Well done on making it the final chapter of the book. After reading through the action-based pointers in each chapter, there is little to say. I have shared everything I understand and know about. I hope this book has given you valuable insights that help you lead a more harmonious life.

Building a harmonious family life requires continuous effort, patience, understanding, and love. Recognizing and addressing each family member's unique needs can create an environment of mutual respect, support, and happiness.

About the Author

Sheetal Kumar Niranjan is an Indian Author, an eco-enthusiast and an I.T. professional with 16 years of experience. He currently works at Tesco Bengaluru as a Systems Engineer. He holds a Master's degree in Electrical Engineering from State University of New York, New Paltz, U.S.A. and a Bachelor's degree in Electronics and Communication Engineering from B.M.S. Institute of Technology, Bangalore, India.

He loves to explore food and try different delicacies from various cuisines. An avid sports lover and enthusiast, he likes to both watch and play sports. He loves playing cricket and foosball. He also loves to travel and watch movies that inspire him. His recent interest has been in researching and learning about climate change and the impact it's causing around the world. He also loves to understand about relationships in life and through this book, he shares his learnings and knowledge with the readers.

You can reach out to him at sheetalkumarn@gmail.com with your reviews and thoughts.

Books by this Author

ECO-LIVING STARTS AT HOME: 10 Ways to Go Green Today

The idea for writing "Eco-Living Starts at Home" came as i was exploring options to live a more sustainable lifestyle and by looking to make changes at home that would support this lifestyle. Not only was i looking for ways to reduce our carbon footprint but i was also looking to save money by doing so.

If you are somebody like me who is ready to positively impact our planet by heading toward living a sustainable lifestyle, then "Eco-Living Starts at Home" is your guide. This e-book is packed with practical tips, budget-friendly options and solutions that provide a clear roadmap to help you make changes in your life and contribute to building a more sustainable future.

Inside the e-book, you will find out about

- How to assess your environmental impact.
- Ways to reduce energy consumption.

- Use of renewable sources to generate clean energy.
- Water conservation practices.
- Waste reduction and recycling.
- Sustainable options to construct or renovate homes.
- Sustainable transportation choices.
- Use of eco-friendly personal hygiene & cleaning products.
- Green gardening & landscaping practices.
- Most importantly, building eco-conscious habits that would make you want to live a sustainable lifestyle.

Get your copy of "Eco-Living Starts at Home" today and embark on your journey towards a greener, more sustainable lifestyle.

Amazon -> https://amzn.to/3yrwv4A

www.ingramcontent.com/pod-product-compliance
Lightning Source LLC
Chambersburg PA
CBHW020506160726

47991CB00007B/2832